BEGINNING DJEMBE

ESSENTIAL TONES, RHYTHMS, & GROOVES

To access video visit:
www.halleonard.com/mylibrary

Enter Code
4852-4362-8060-9171

D0584824

BY MICHAEL MARKUS WITH JOE GALEOTA

BERKLEE PRESS

Editor in Chief: Jonathan Feist
Senior Vice President of Online Learning and Continuing Education/CEO of Berklee Online: Debbie Cavalier
Assistant Vice President of Marketing and Recruitment for Berklee Media: Mike King
Dean of Continuing Education: Carin Nuernberg
Editorial Assistants: Emily Jones, Eloise Kelsey
Notation Assistant: John Doing
Video Director: Mark Freed
Cover by Kathy Kikkert
Instruments and Still Photos Provided by Wula Drum

ISBN 978-0-87639-168-6

Berklee Press

1140 Boylston Street
Boston, MA 02215-3693 USA
(617) 747-2146

Visit Berklee Press Online at
www.berkleepress.com

Berklee Online

online.berklee.edu

DISTRIBUTED BY

HAL•LEONARD®
CORPORATION
7777 W. BLUEMOUND RD. P.O. BOX 13819
MILWAUKEE, WISCONSIN 53213

Visit Hal Leonard Online
www.halleonard.com

Berklee Press, a publishing activity of Berklee College of Music, is a not-for-profit educational publisher.
Available proceeds from the sales of our products are contributed to the scholarship funds of the college.

CONTENTS

ABOUT THE VIDEOS

To access the accompanying videos, go to www.halleonard.com/mylibrary and enter the code found on the first page of this book. This will grant you instant access to every example. Examples with accompanying videos are marked with a video icon.

The accompanying videos can be used independently, in sequence, or in conjunction with this book.

PART I

Introduction to the Djembe

Traditionally, within West African culture, the djembe is played for several reasons. Mostly, it is played for celebration, to accompany the dance, and even communicate. There are hundreds of traditional rhythms that are played on the djembe. It is woven into the fabric of the culture, the people, the language, and the customs. For example, when farmers work (by hand, no machines), the drummers play to help create inspiration, motivation, and a steady beat to work by.

As in all cultures, music in Guinea is important for marking any significant time of life: marriage, the harvest, a baby naming, and also a special figure in the community, the hunters, rites of passage, the women, the men, the young, the elderly, history, etc. Most often, along with the music, there is dance, and the lead drummer's primary role is to follow the dancer, marking their step.

The djembe is a call to the community. It brings people together and communicates to people in the area that something special is happening. On a special day, there may be a parade led by the drummer, or a performance to let people know that something important is about to happen, or that a visitor is approaching soon.

Origins

The djembe originated in West Africa—mainly Guinea, Mali, Cote d'Ivoire, and Burkina Faso. Within each of these countries, there are many different ethnic groups, or "tribes." Each has a distinct language, style of dress, cuisine, music, and history that is slightly different than the others.

At first, the music may seem the same. However, after studying it a bit, you will notice the different dialect or accent within each style. Even within the same country, the differentiation between styles is immense. One can study it for one's entire lifetime and only scratch the surface. In Guinea alone, there are over fifteen different languages spoken, and all have different rhythms, dances, and customs.

So how did the djembe come to us?

This music was first made popular in the West during the 1950s through the "ballets," which are professional ensembles that depict their culture on stage. Just as in the European ballet, the African ensembles create stories, or "programs," which demonstrate African culture through story, song, and dance. Most ballets were formed in the cities, where there were more artists and people to help support them. The directors started with the traditional forms (from the village), and then expounded upon them to make them faster, more complicated, and more exciting for the stage. The village (traditional) is the orgin of the music, and the ballet (contemporary) made it popular through performance and touring worldwide, exposing foreigners to the wonderful world of African Arts.

The ballet brought together the best artists from each village so that everyone could learn each others' cultures. Before this, the music did not travel far outside each village.

Griot System

A "griot" is a person from a caste system, born into a specific family name, who keeps the oral history. Griots are keepers of the oral history, mythology, folklore, songs, and the movement of specific families from their region. Much like the blacksmiths, or "wandering minstrels" in European culture, the information was handed down grandfather, to father, to child, to grandchild—an oral tradition. Instruments within the griot families of West Africa include the kora, the balaphone, and the singing voice.

The djembe is *not* a griot instrument. This is why no one knows the exact history of the rhythms, as we know the history of the songs. However, the master drummers and professional artists help keep the traditional rhythms correct.

Each rhythm does have a place of origin. When in Africa, I always learned specific rhythms from the teachers who were from the area of the rhythms they taught, or travelled to that area to learn. That way, I was getting the music more directly and a bit closer to the "true" origin.

In the videos and in the last part of this book, we will explore rhythms from the different regions of Guinea. First, though, let's look at djembe technique and some exercises that will help you to achieve a good djembe sound.

1. NOTATION AND KEY

In this book, we will use the following conventions for notation. Examples will use both traditional and graphic notation. Note: *Dundun* include kenkeni, sangban, and dundunba.

Traditional Notation

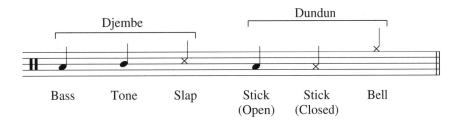

FIG. 1.1. Traditional Notation

Graphic Notation

In the graphical notation, each set of adjacent squares in the same shade is a beat, and each square is a subdivision of the beat. Letters indicate the djembe sounds.

Djembes:

Slap	S
Tone	T
Bass	B

Dunduns:

Bell	X
Stick (Open)	O
Stick (Closed)	C

FIG. 1.2. Graphical Notation

2. TECHNIQUE

The djembe can be played either in a sitting or standing position. As with playing any instrument, it is important to be relaxed.

Sitting Position

When sitting at the djembe, make sure you are seated somewhat forward in your chair so that your legs can reach around the drum and your arms are free to move up and down. The djembe is played evenly with both hands, so sitting straight with your weight balanced is best. Keep your posture straight but not rigid. You do not want your shoulders rounded, as this will prevent you from full range of motion of your arms.

It is best to look straight ahead, rather than keeping your head down all the time. Looking up, eventually, after you have learned the hand placements, is better for concentration as well as posture.

Drum Position

Tilt your drum forward, away from you. This enables the air to flow underneath it so that you can produce a good bass sound. Also, it will project the sound away from you and prevent any possible jamming of the wrist. Angling the drum properly will ensure a good tone and slap, as long as you rebound off the skin and do not stifle the sound.

Standing Position

Standing with the djembe is like playing a whole new instrument. It is best to first learn sitting position before attempting to play while standing. And because playing the djembe is very physical, you must be careful when standing.

It is best to use one strap that goes around your shoulders, across your back, and around the drum. Some people only put a strap around the waist, but this can put extra pressure on the back.

While maintaining a good upright posture, adjust the drum's height. It should not be so high that it is tight against the groin or so low that it is hard to reach, or encourages you to slouch and disrupts your good posture. Playing with it at the wrong height could lead to back injury.

Also consider the length of space between the strap and the drum. The drum should remain at a good playing angle, and not become like a tabletop.

Everyone is a little different, in both preference and in arm and torso length. So, experiment with the exact level of the djembe in relation to your body. Some people use their arms more, some their wrists more.

Hand Stretches

As with any physical activity, it is important to warm up. Here are some easy stretches for the fingers, wrists, forearms, and shoulders. Warm-up stretches should be gentle, slow, and gradual. There should not be pain or straining involved, as this is jarring to the muscles and tendons, and anti-productive. Some good, basic exercises are presented in the videos and in chapter 5.

3. HOW TO MAKE THE THREE SOUNDS OF THE DJEMBE

There are three main sounds played on the djembe: the bass, tone, and slap.

The Bass

The *bass* is the lowest sound, made by playing in the middle of the drum. The whole hand strikes the drum in an open position and bounces off the skin so the drum can ring out. Again, tilt the drum forward to let the air move. Otherwise, it will not sound.

The Tone

The *tone* is the middle-pitched sound. This sound is made by placing the fingers together, except the thumb; the thumb is at a right angle to the hand. Place the hand on the edge of the drum, with the entire length of the fingers on the drum. Avoid slamming your hand into the wood edge; play over the open part of the skin, on top. Move your hand all the way in so that even the pinky's bottom knuckle is on the drum. Remember, the thumb does not really touch the drum. And just like the bass, bounce the hand off the drum to enable it to sing. Focus on the "pad" of the hand, as this is its strongest, thickest part.

The Slap

Many people are drawn to the slap sound because it is the highest pitched. However, it does not have to be the loudest. When listening to a professional play, you will notice that the slap does not have to be louder than the tone; it is just a higher pitch. My own tone may be louder than my slap.

While keeping the same position as used in the tone, simply open your fingers a little bit. Make sure the hand is relaxed, but not too relaxed, and not too stiff.

All Sounds

All the sounds are made by moving from the elbow. The wrist is flexible but not too loose. It is more about the forearm moving from the elbow.

Every time you play a note, you must rebound off the drum.

Think of your arm like a drum stick. Let the drum ring out and be heard, and always lift off the drum. This is more important than slamming down onto the drum.

You do *not* have to play hard; just lift off the skin. This should produce a pleasant sound.

All your fingers need to strike the drum at the same time, as one mechanism. With practice, you can find that a lot of sound can be produced without playing hard by "scooping" the sound out of the drum.

And *always* relax and breathe.

4. THE ENSEMBLE

The Break

7

The *lead* drummer "speaks" to the ensemble and gives cues, sets tempos, and guides the group. In order to do this without talking or counting, the lead drummer plays a phrase called the "break."

The break is the signal played to start, stop, or change musicians. It also tells the dancer(s) to change their step, and it sets the tempo.

Traditionally, there is no exact break played. It is more of an improvised phrase accented by the lead drummer to encourage the dancer to change.

The break warns of when to end the song, and how to end cleanly by the ensemble stopping together. Pre-set breaks became more popular because of the ballets (ensembles), as when performing choreography, the dancers needed to know when to change, as a group. The lead drummer usually plays the highest pitched drum, thus queuing others by "speaking" using their instrument.

Over the years, specific breaks have started being played for each rhythm. Some rhythms have unique breaks that only fit that rhythm. Others can be a general break that is used in many rhythms that fit a specific time signature.

Here is an example of the most common break for 4/4 rhythms for the djembe.

Break

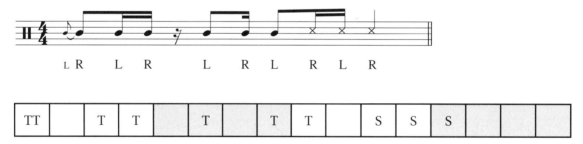

FIG. 4.1. Example Djembe Break: Sofa. See page 3 for a drum key.

The Djembe Accompaniments

Each rhythm has two or three djembe accompaniment patterns. Accompaniments are the repetitive patterns played by each of the djembes. Drummers playing accompaniments do not improvise or offer variations, but repeat and keep the tempo. The role is similar to the rhythm guitar; it's the "motor" of the music.

Accompanists do not accent. The syncopation of slap, tone, and bass of all the parts together creates a sense of phrasing. Learning the accompaniment is necessary to learn how to play for the dancer or to solo, as these patterns teach endurance, form the specific nuances of each rhythm, shape the feeling, and make each rhythm unique unto itself. Some accompaniments will be downbeat oriented, some are upbeat, and each accompaniment drum should be tuned differently so that the parts together make up the whole song.

Dunduns

The bass drums of the ensemble are called the *dunduns*. Within the ensemble, there are usually three dunduns: the dundunba (biggest), the sangban (middle), and the kenkeni (smallest).

Dunduns are made of a solid piece of wood, shaped as cylinders. They are mounted with cow skins and played with sticks.

Traditionally, there is one player per drum, and a bell on each instrument. This creates three drum tones and three differently pitched bells, all working together at the same time. In more contemporary styles, one person can play all three drums, turned over, like a drum set.

Lead Drummer

The lead drummer has an important role and several main tasks in the ensemble.

He or she commands the tempo of the music, the starting and stopping queues, and any signals for changes in the music or elaborate arrangements. Most importantly, the lead drummer plays for the dancer by marking their steps and keeping up the energy for them.

He or she basically guides the listeners' ears to different points of the music and keeps the music energetic and in control.

This video shows the djembe improvising in a performance context. The rest of the book will provide exercises and typical rhythms of the djembe ensemble, so that you can create your own similar performances.

PART II

Exercises for Sounds and Subdivisions

These exercises will help you learn to play the three sounds on the djembe: bass, tone, and slap.

It is important to isolate each sound by itself and to practice changing sounds, all in a methodical, organized manner. In order to do so, it is helpful to separate from any specific rhythm; just keep a basic pulse, and play the even subdivisions of the beat.

Binary time means there are four subdivisions per beat.

Ternary time means there are three subdivisions per beat.

Keep track of where the "one" is by tapping your foot, or saying "one," or just feeling it. Especially for the "Drop One" or "Drop Two" exercises, keeping track of the pulse will instill a solid sense of rhythmic confidence and enable you to hold the beat at any tempo.

In addition, make sure you play as even-handedly as possible. Always alternate, and be sure to give equal attention to both the right and the left hands.

Repeat each exercise over and over. First start with your right hand, then start with your left hand, and alternate hands every stroke.

Key

B = Bass
T = Tone
S = Slap

Ternary: Three Subdivisions per Beat

1	2	3

Binary: Four Subdivisions per Beat

1	2	3	4

5. PRACTICE ROUTINE

The exercises in this chapter are some of my favorites, comprising what I consider an essential djembe practice routine, particularly for a beginning player. You can watch me go through this set on the videos. Then, the following chapters present additional exercises to give you greater control over your sound, technique, and sense of rhythm.

Exercise 5.1. Basic Exercise

10

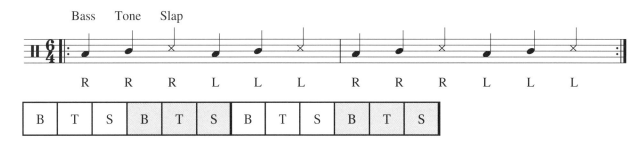

Exercise 5.2. Binary Exercise 1

11

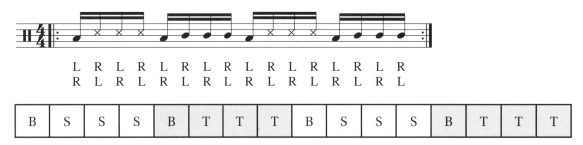

Exercise 5.3. Binary Exercise 2

12

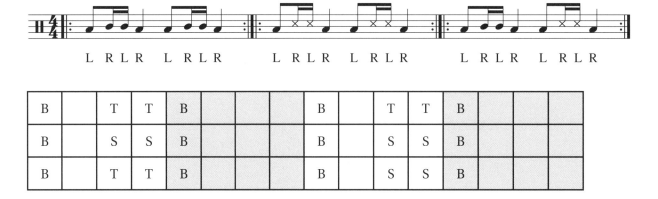

Exercise 5.4. Binary Exercise 3

13

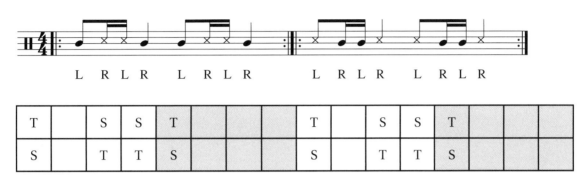

L R L R   L R L R   L R L R   L R L R

T		S	S	T				T		S	S	T			
S		T	T	S				S		T	T	S			

Exercise 5.5. Rolls

14

R L   R L
L R   L R

R L   R L   R L R L R L   R L R L R L
L R   L R   L R L R L R   L R L R L R

Exercise 5.6. Ternary Exercise 1

15

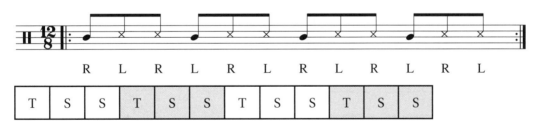

R L R L R L R L R L R L

T	S	S	T	S	S	T	S	S	T	S	S

Exercise 5.7. Ternary Exercise 2

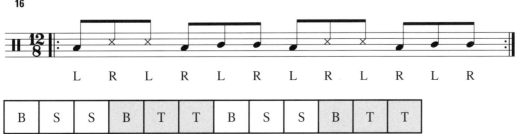
16

L R L R L R L R L R L R

B	S	S	B	T	T	B	S	S	B	T	T

Exercise 5.8. Ternary Exercise 3

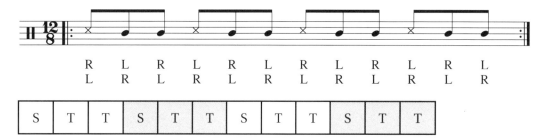

S	T	T	S	T	T	S	T	T	S	T	T

Exercise 5.9. Swing Feel

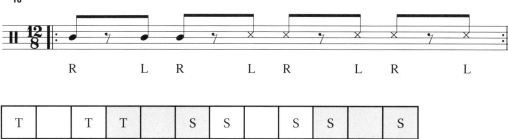

T		T	T		S	S		S	S		S

6. ISOLATION EXERCISES

In chapters 6 to 9, each row can be interpreted either as a beat (with subdivisions) or as a measure (with beats). Practice each row independently, repeating it over and over. In this chapter's isolation exercises, alternate each stroke, and keep every strike steady and even.

Binary

Exercise 6.1. One Note

B	B	B	B

T	T	T	T

S	S	S	S

Exercise 6.2. One Sound vs. Three

B	S	S	S

S	B	S	S

S	S	B	S

S	S	S	B

B	T	T	T

T	B	T	T

T	T	B	T

T	T	T	B

S	B	B	B

B	S	B	B

B	B	S	B

B	B	B	S

T	S	S	S

S	T	S	S

S	S	T	S

S	S	S	T

S	T	T	T

T	S	T	T

T	T	S	T

T	T	T	S

T	B	B	B

B	T	B	B

B	B	T	B

B	B	B	T

Exercise 6.3. Two vs. Two

B	B	S	S

S	S	B	B

B	S	B	S

S	B	S	B

S	B	B	S

B	S	S	B

B	B	T	T

T	T	B	B

B	T	B	T

T	B	T	B

T	B	B	T

B	T	T	B

S	S	T	T

T	T	S	S

S	T	S	T

T	S	T	S

T	S	S	T

S	T	T	S

Exercise 6.4. Three Sounds

| B | B | T | S |

| B | B | S | T |

| T | S | B | B |

| S | T | B | B |

| B | T | B | S |

| B | S | B | T |

| B | T | S | B |

| B | S | T | B |

| T | B | B | S |

| S | B | B | T |

| T | B | S | B |

| S | B | T | B |

| T | T | B | S |

| T | T | S | B |

| B | S | T | T |

| S | B | T | T |

| T | B | T | S |

| T | S | T | B |

T	B	S	T

T	S	B	T

B	T	T	S

S	T	T	B

B	T	S	T

S	T	B	T

S	S	B	T

S	S	T	B

T	B	S	S

B	T	S	S

S	B	S	T

S	T	S	B

S	B	T	S

S	T	B	S

B	S	S	T

T	S	S	B

B	S	T	S

T	S	B	S

Ternary

Exercise 6.5. One Sound

B	B	B
T	T	T
S	S	S

Exercise 6.6. Two Sounds

B	S	S

B	B	S

S	S	B

S	B	B

S	B	S

B	S	B

B	T	T

B	B	T

T	T	B

T	B	B

T	B	T

B	T	B

S	T	T

S	S	T

S	T	S

T	S	S

T	T	S

T	S	T

Exercise 6.7. Three Sounds: Bass, Tone, Slap

A. Ternary 1

B	T	S
B	S	T
T	S	B

B. Ternary 2

T	B	S
S	T	B
S	B	T

7. "DROP ONE" BALANCING EXERCISES

Binary

Exercise 7.1. Drop One: Bass

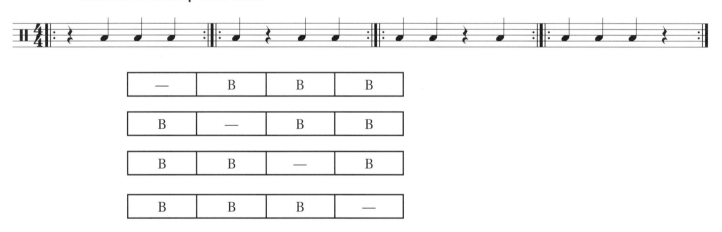

—	B	B	B
B	—	B	B
B	B	—	B
B	B	B	—

Exercise 7.2. Drop One: Tone

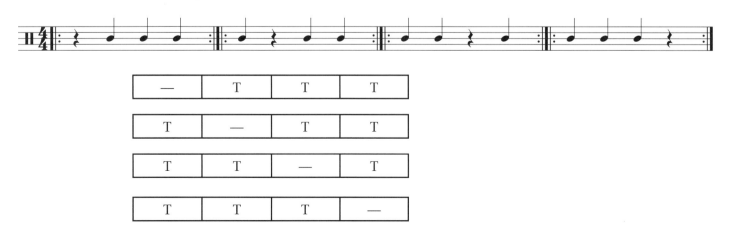

—	T	T	T
T	—	T	T
T	T	—	T
T	T	T	—

Exercise 7.3. Drop One: Slap

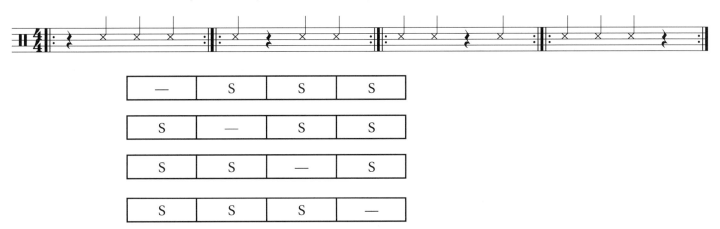

—	S	S	S

S	—	S	S

S	S	—	S

S	S	S	—

Ternary

Exercise 7.4. Three Tones: Bass, Tone, Slap

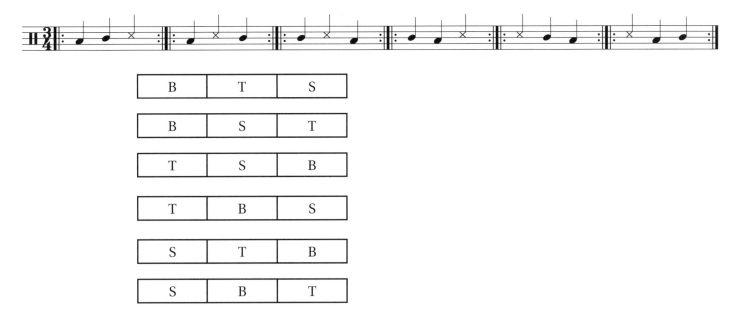

B	T	S

B	S	T

T	S	B

T	B	S

S	T	B

S	B	T

8. "DROP TWO" BALANCING EXERCISES
Binary

Exercise 8.1. Drop Two: Bass

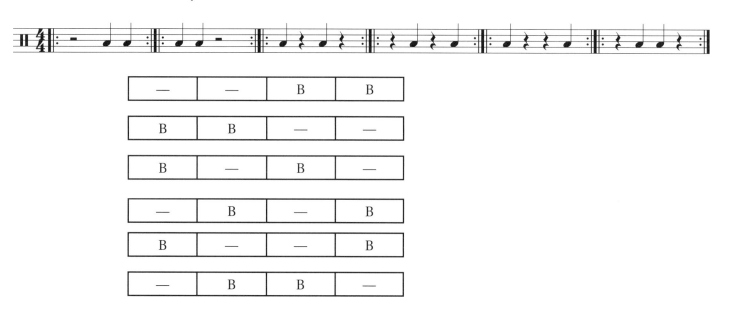

Exercise 8.2. Drop Two: Tone

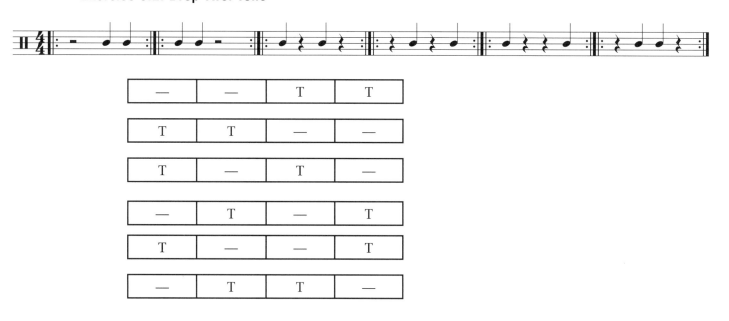

Exercise 8.3. Drop Two: Slap

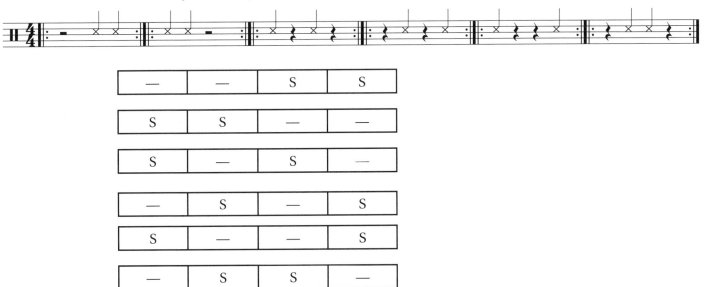

| — | — | S | S |

| S | S | — | — |

| S | — | S | — |

| — | S | — | S |

| S | — | — | S |

| — | S | S | — |

Ternary

Exercise 8.4. Drop Two: One Note

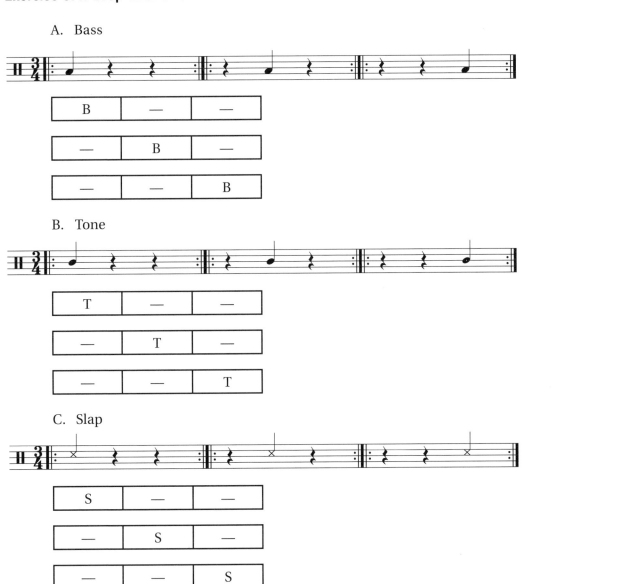

A. Bass

| B | — | — |

| — | B | — |

| — | — | B |

B. Tone

| T | — | — |

| — | T | — |

| — | — | T |

C. Slap

| S | — | — |

| — | S | — |

| — | — | S |

9. "DROP THREE" BALANCING EXERCISES (BINARY)

Exercise 9.1. Drop Three: Bass

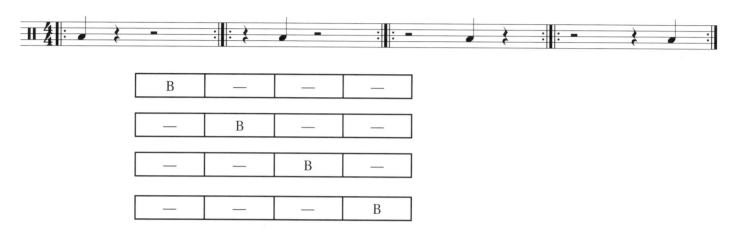

Exercise 9.2. Drop Three: Tone

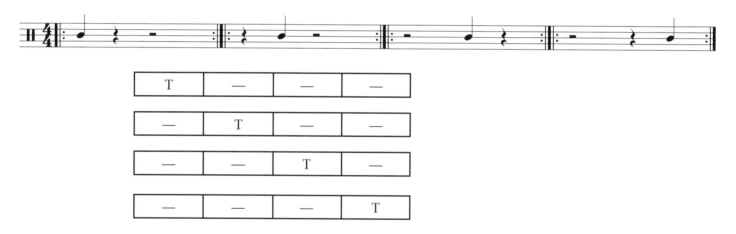

Exercise 9.3. Drop Three: Slap

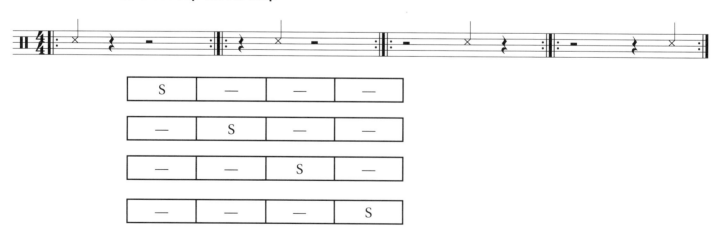

PART III

The Rhythms of Guinea

10. NATURAL REGIONS OF GUINEA

The "natural" regions of Guinea are:

- Upper
- Maritime (Coastal)
- Forest
- Fouta Djallon (Middle)

Each of these regions has different "tribes" and different music.

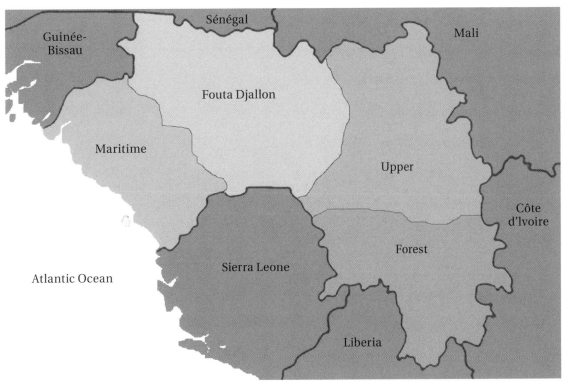

FIG. 10.1. Natural Regions of Guinea

Guinea is a lush country with most of it covered by forest, unlike the neighboring countries such as Senegal and Mali, which have more desert. Guinea is rich in minerals, gold, diamonds, and most of all, bauxite (aluminum).

Although the djembe is popular all throughout Guinea, it is played differently in each region.

In Upper Guinea, the Maninka people's djembe ensemble includes two or three djembes with two or three dunduns.

In Maritime (Coastal) Guinea, the djembe ensemble often has a bass djembe, and the dunduns are played upright and without the bells, or with no dunduns at all.

In the forest region, the djembe is used in conjunction with the krin, or kyrin (log drum). They also have different sized djembes tied together called "forest djembe," which includes one medium or small djembe with four to five baby djembes tied to it. One drummer can play a series of melodic variations.

In the Fouta Djallon, the djembe can be used to accompany many different instruments, such as the one-string violin, the kula flute, the wassakumba, or the guitar.

The djembe is more of an accompanying instrument rather than the main focus.

11. RHYTHM EXAMPLES FROM EACH REGION

Here are some examples of the rich variety of rhythms throughout Guinea. We have chosen at least one rhythm per main area of the country.

Sofa (Upper Guinea)

Sofa is from Upper Guinea in the Kouroussa region. It is played as a celebration dance in preparation for a hunt. Sofa was likely inspired by a rhythm played on the bolon, which is a bass harp.

Break

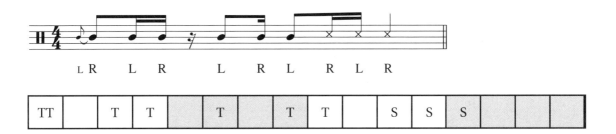

Ensemble

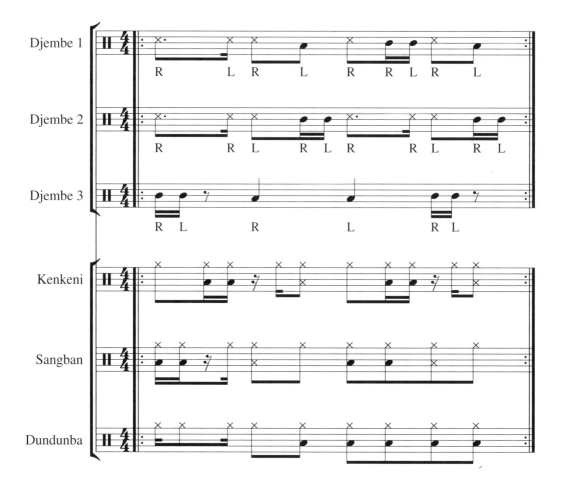

Djembe 1

S			S	S		B	S		T	T	S		B	

Djembe 2

S			S	S		T	T	S			S	S		T	T

Djembe 3

T	T			B			B				T	T	

Kenkeni

X		X	X		X	X		X		X	X		X	X	
		O	O			C				O	O			C	

Sangban

X	X		X	X		X		X		X		X		X	
O	O			C				O		O		C			

Dundunba

X	X		X	X		X		X		X		X		X	
					O		O		O		O		O	

Dundungbe (Upper Guinea)

Dundungbe, one of the dundunba rhythms, comes from Kouroussa. The ballet created additional accompaniments, but traditionally, Djembe 2 was the only accompaniment.

Break

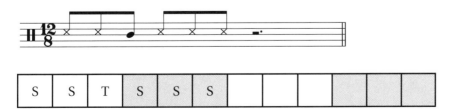

S	S	T	S	S	S						

Ensemble

Djembe 1

						S			S	T	T	S			S	T	T	S			S	T	T	S			S	T	T

S				S	T	T	S			S	T	T	S			S	T	T	S			S	T	T

Djembe 2

						S		T	S			S		T	S			S		T	S			S		T	S		

S		T	S			S		T	S			S		T	S			S		T	S		

Djembe 3

						T	T					T	T	B				T	T					T	T	B		B	

T	T					T	T	B				T	T					T	T	B			B	

Kenkeni

	X		X	X	X		X		X	X	X		X		X	X	X		X		X	X	X		X		X	X
	O		O	O			O		O	O			O		O	O			O		O	O			O		O	O

X		X	X	X	X		X		X	X	X	X		X		X	X	X	X		X		X	X
	O		O	O			O		O	O			O		O	O			O		O	O	

Sangban

	X		X		X		X	X		X		X	X		X		X		X	X		X		X	X		X	
	O				C							O		C						O								

X		X		X		X	X		X		X		X	X		X	X		X		X		
	O		O		O			O			C							O					

Dundunba

	X	X		X	X		X	X		X	X		X	X		X	X		X	X		X	X		X	X
	O	O		O	O								O	O		O	O							O	O		O	O

X		X		X		X	X		X	X		X	X		X	X		X	X		X	X
	O		O		O		O	O									O	O		O	O	

Soli (Throughout Guinea)

Soli is a rhythm from the Mandinka (or Malinke) people. It is used throughout all of Guinea, with many regional variations. It is used to celebrate a boy's initiation into manhood.

Break

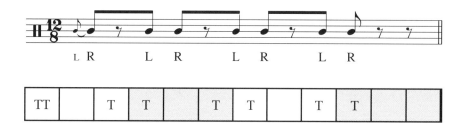

Ensemble

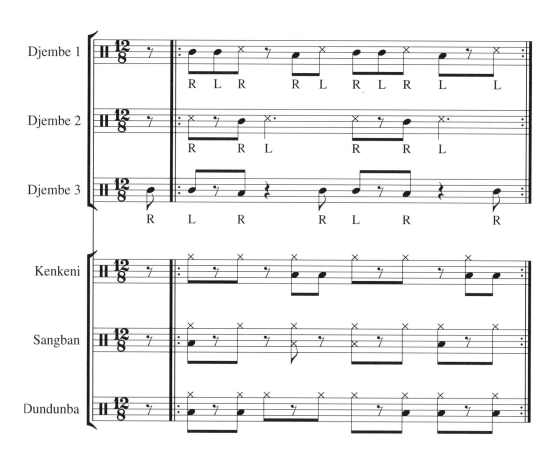

Djembe 1

	T	T	S		B	S	T	T	S	B		S

Djembe 2

	S		T	S			S		T	S		

Djembe 3

T	T		B			T	T		B			T

Kenkeni

	X		X		X		X		X		X	
					O	O					O	O

Sangban

	X		X		X		X		X	X		X
	O				C		C			O		

Dundunba

	X		X	X		X	X		X	X		X
	O		O						O	O		O

Guinea Fare (Coastal Guinea)

Guinea means "woman" and *fare* means "dance." Guinea fare is danced by women at all happy occasions, particularly at bridal showers.

Break

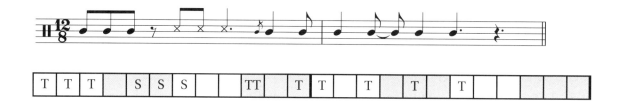

| T | T | T | S | S | S | | TT | T | T | | T | | T | | T | | | | |

Ensemble

Djembe 1

		B	S		B	T		S	S		T	T			S			T		S	S		T	T		B

Djembe 2

		B	S		B	T	T		S			T	T		S			T	T		S			T		B

Djembe 3

		B	S		B			T	T					S				T	T				B

Kenkeni

			X		X		X		X	X		X	X		X		X		X	X		X
			C				O		O			C			O		O			O		

Sangban

			S			S			S			S			S			S			S			S	
						O						O						O						O	

Dundunba

			X		X		X		X	X		X		X	X		X		X		X	X		X		X
		O	O																							O

Kuku (Forest)

Kuku comes from the village of Beyla. It is music for the celebration of fishermen returning from the river with their catch.

Break

Ensemble

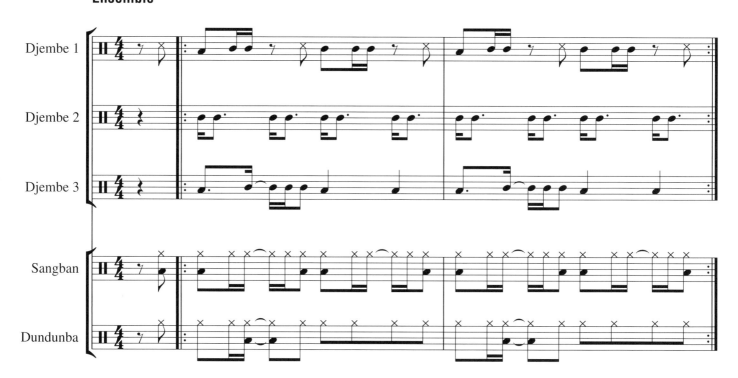

Djembe 1

		S		B		T	T			S		T		T	T			S	

B		T	T			S		T		T	T			S	

Djembe 2

				T	T			T	T			T	T			T	T		

T	T			T	T			T	T			T	T		

Djembe 3

				B			T		T	T		B				B			

B			T		T	T		B				B			

Sangban

		X		X		X	X			X	X		X		X	X		X	X	
		O		O							O		O						O	

X		X	X			X	X		X		X	X			X	X	
O						O			O							O	

Dundunba

		X		X		X	X			X		X		X		X		X	
							O												

X		X	X			X		X		X		X		X	
			O												

Mane (Guinea Fare)

Traditionally played on the Balafon (xylophone) without many djembes, mane is another women's dance from the Guinea Fare family of rhythms. It comes from the Susu people, and is played for weddings, celebrations, and coming together.

Break

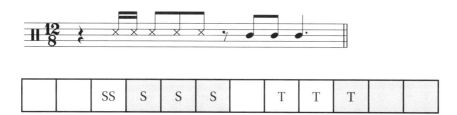

Ensemble

Djembe 1

					S	B	T		S	S	S		T		S	S	S		T		S	S	S		T	T		B

Djembe 2

					T		S	S	T	S			S	S	T	S	T		S	S	T	S			S	S	T	S

Djembe 3

					T	T	B			T	T	B			T	T	B			T	T	B		

Kenkeni

					X		X	X		X	X		X	X		X	X		X	X		X	X		X	X		X
								O			O			O			O			O			O			O			O

Sangban

					X		X		X		X		X		X		X		X		X		X		X	
							O		O				O		O				O		O				O		O	

Dundunba

X	X	X		X		X		X	X		X	X		X	X		X	X		X	X	X	X		X	
O	O	O		O		O															O	O	O		O	

Sinte (Coastal Guinea)

The rhythm sinte is from the Nalo ethnic group in the village of Boke. It is traditionally played on the krin (log drum). My teacher M'bemba Bangoura transposed the rhythms from krin to the djembe ensemble and created this break.

Break

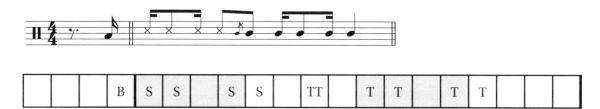

Ensemble

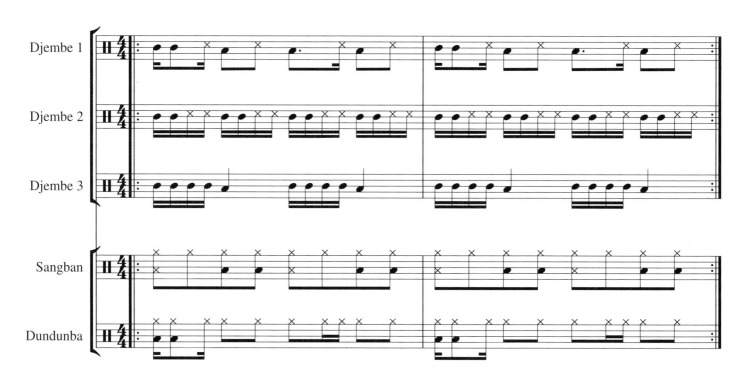

Djembe 1

T	T		S	B		S		B			S	B		S	

Djembe 2

T	T	S	S	T	T	S	S	T	T	S	S	T	T	S	S

Djembe 3

T	T	T	T	B				T	T	T	T	B			

Sangban

X		X		X		X		X		X		X		Ẋ	
C				O		O		C				O		O	

Dundunba

S	S		S	S		S		S	S	S		S		S	
O	O														

ABOUT THE AUTHOR

21

As a musician, artistic director, and educator, **Michael Markus** has spent over twenty years performing, teaching, and studying West African drumming. Along with a BFA in percussion, he has mentored with accomplished master indigenous artists and travels often to Guinea to learn more.

He has co-produced and released a CD of his previous group, Magbana, as well as a series of eleven educational percussion CDs, plus a DVD of master drummers from Guinea. As a world music clinician, he has presented at versatile venues ranging from college music and dance departments to inner city community centers. He has regularly developed and conducted workshops for national and international percussion conventions, master classes at various universities and public and private schools all over the United States, Canada, and Mexico. He has also created commissioned pieces, composing and directing choreography for such groups as Ethos Percussion, which debuted his work at the Symphony Space in New York City.

Michael is dedicated to the preservation and promotion of cultural arts and socioeconomic development in Guinea, West Africa, where he has based the production end of his company, Wula Drum, where authentically elegant and professional sounding African drums are crafted.

Recently, Michael has become department chair at the Brooklyn School of Music, where he started The World Percussion Center of New York, a school dedicated to represent education of all hand-percussion instruments worldwide.

INDEX

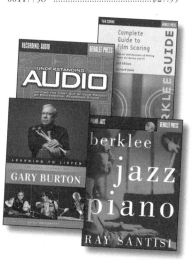

0316